Adjusting, Adapting, and Managing Expectations of Overseas Basketball

Dominique Johnson

Copyright © 2022 Dominique Johnson

ISBN: 979-8-9864426-0-0

All Rights Reserved. No part of this publication may be reproduced or transmitted, stored in a retrieval system, or transmitted in any form or by any means, electronic, mechanical, photocopying, recording, scanning, or otherwise, except as permitted by law, without prior written permission of the author.

Printed in the United States of America

Editor: Sharp Editorial

Cover design and format: Chynna Creative Co

Dedication

This basketball business is very shady, and I would not be where I am today if it weren't for my agent, mentor, and brother, Craig McKenzie. You opened my eyes so much about this game but, more importantly, life. Because of you, I am a better man, husband, and leader, and the list goes on. This book is truly dedicated to you because without your guidance and the first of many phone conversations we had about God, I do not know where I would be.

Acknowledgments

To my wife, Marissa Johnson: You have stuck with me through thick and thin, and this overseas journey has been a real-life roller coaster, but you've been right next to me the entire ride. This book is not possible without your support and everlasting love. So, thank you!

To all of my teammates that I've had throughout my career: I can't thank you guys enough for all of the good times we've had and the blood, sweat, and tears we shared on the court. Thank you as well.

To my best friend, Dwayne Lackey: All of those late-night calls talking about the good, the bad, and the ugly were more help than you think. You are also a part of this book, and I can't thank you enough for being there for me when I needed you.

To someone that showed me how to make it out of the neighborhood the right way, Donnie Calvin. You gave me the inspiration to write this book and actually follow through with it. I hope I make you proud when you read it, and hopefully, it can inspire the next kid from our neighborhood to pursue greatness. Thank you.

Last but not least, my parents, Clyde and Eloise Johnson: You have been there for me through day one, and even if you did not understand some of the things I was going through in this journey, your support for me never wavered. I'm glad I got the chance to share some of these memories with you and see the look of proudness on your faces as I looked at you from the floor into the stands. Thank you!

A Note to the Reader

The information I share in this book is *not* to deter you or anyone from achieving a life-long dream. However, I am sharing this information to prepare you for the many unknowns that await once you embark on the journey of playing professional basketball overseas. I have been blessed to play for ten-plus years, winning championships, MVP titles, and securing all-star spots, and I want to share the knowledge I've gained from my experiences. Some of these stories are encouraging, inspiring, and uplifting; others are shocking, discouraging, and downright unbelievable. Fortunately for you, my mistakes have already been made. The purpose of *Adjusting, Adapting, and Managing Expectations of Overseas Basketball* is to ensure you do not repeat my mistakes because most of my mistakes are avoidable. Dismiss any preconceived ideas you may have about playing basketball abroad. Buckle up because you're about to experience some heavy turbulence, but success is waiting for you when you land.

Table of Contents

INTRODUCTION	1
CHAPTER 1: AGENTS	7
CHAPTER 2: MUST-KNOW CONTRACT INFORMATION	16
CHAPTER 3: ARRIVING IN EUROPE	23
CHAPTER 4: MANAGING YOUR MONEY	29
CHAPTER 5: LET'S TALK MONEY	36
CHAPTER 6: PROTECTING YOURSELF	43
CHAPTER 7: OVERSEAS BASKETBALL	48
CHAPTER 8: MENTAL HEALTH	54
CHAPTER 9: LEISURE	63
CHAPTER 10: EXTRAS	69
CONCLUSION	75

Introduction

Nearly a decade ago, on December 30, 2012, I played my first professional season in Poland. This was my first year abroad, and our team was set to play the second leg of our derby game against Anwil at their home arena. This was the first time my then-girlfriend, now wife, had been overseas with me, and we had no idea what to expect when playing a rival game on the road.

When you think of rival basketball games, the Lakers vs. Celtics probably come to mind. And when you think of the environment of that rival game, you already know what to expect: fans booing loudly, especially at the free-throw line, some heckling and shouting at the opposing team, and attendees decked out in their respective team's colors. The atmosphere is hype, and people are ready for what is sure to be an intense matchup.

Well, rivalries overseas are not as... *expected*.

Our team was to leave one day before the game so that we could be there on time, prepare, and get a good night's rest.

My girlfriend and the other players' partners were to arrive at Anwil on the day of the game.

With full-on police escorts protecting and guiding the girlfriends and wives inside the arena, Marissa, my girlfriend, quickly discovered that rivalries are not as friendly overseas. As my teammates and I went through pre-game warm-ups and Marissa sat in the stands, a wave of shock rushed over me. Fans were throwing objects on the court, completely ignoring the warnings of security. They were lighting flairs in the stands, taunting opposing fans to incite a fight, and laughing as their children shouted curse words at the players. Drums and horns blared from the fan sections, drowning out the warm-up music in the arena. The vibe was hostile, and the normalcy of intense competition was obsolete.

This chaos was my new normal.

This was overseas basketball.

That night, we lost by 18 points. Truth be told, I'm surprised we didn't lose by more because the club had just fired our coach before the game, and the assistant coach, Jerzy Chudeusz, had taken over for the remainder of the year. Despite the circumstances, I hate losing, especially to our rival team and by a large margin.

Two days after the game, practice resumed, but before we hit the court, we were told to go to the video room because the president wanted to speak with us.

"What could this be about?" I wondered, assuming we would get a lecture or two about the loss or a pep talk about the new coaching staff.

As we entered the room, I could sense something was off by the uncomfortable body language of my teammates, but I had no idea what was about to happen. The president was already sitting in the room with his arms folded and you could damn near see smoke rising from his head. He was pissed, and despite the game being over two days ago, his mood was as if the game had just ended.

As everyone took their seats, the president immediately began to tell us how we played terribly, not fighting for the win. I've come to learn that when your team's president starts to speak English, something is about to go down.

"You disgraced the jersey and shamed the city," he shouted with disgust.

Meanwhile, I was confused. We had lost one game and had a new coach at that, but by the President's fury, you would have thought we lost it all.

With that said, he decided to punish us. I figured we were about to endure some hellish two-a-days or have some extra strength training workout.

Well, my assumption was way off.

Instead, he decided to fine every player $3,000.

Initially, I thought he was threatening us or wanting to keep us on our toes. After all, those types of fines were nowhere in my contract, let alone alluded to, but once I talked to my teammates, I realized this punishment was real, and there was nothing I could do about it. This was the first time I realized that my contract hardly held any weight, that teams could do and say as they pleased with few repercussions.

Next month, true to his word, the president fined each player $3,000. Sadly, that was my entire month's salary. So, there I was, playing for free for an entire month due to the president's imposed fine, but it was certainly not the last time something of that magnitude would transpire.

***

I was born and raised on the east-side of Detroit, Michigan, where basketball was a staple in the community.

Growing up, I was never heavily recruited by the best high schools nor the top Division-1 universities. I traveled a tougher route to reach pro status. However, I am proud to say that I graduated from an NAIA school, Azusa Pacific University, and was one of the few players from the GSAC conference to play at the EuroCup level. That is part of the beauty of overseas basketball—your work ethic will propel your career, not necessarily the reputation of your alma mater. When you look at my university and the elite teams I played on throughout my career, including Umana Reyer Venezia, Alba Berlin, and Banvit Basketbul, you will be amazed because people more than likely counted me out after college.

Nevertheless, the real spotlight is on the information gained during my journey, which will benefit you.

***

Once you secure your first contract, I want you to be well-prepared for anything thrown your way, from not having a vehicle to random fines to what to pack in your luggage. Becoming well-prepared is easier said than done because life throws curveballs, especially in the basketball world, but if you read and digest what I share in this book, you will be ten steps ahead, warranting a much smoother transition to an entirely new world.

Chapter 1

Agents

To the first-year professional basketball athletes reading this book, I want to say congratulations on taking this step into the professional world. I'm sure that the journey you are about to embark on is exciting and perhaps stressful, too.

When I approached the end of my collegiate career, my phone constantly rang with weird area codes from agents whom I had no idea how they got my number. More importantly, beyond not knowing how they got my number, I did not know how to pick an agent.

Every agent I had talked to sounded like the right one but, most of them were not. Only a few athletes will stay with the same agency for the duration of their careers. I was not one of those players. Most of the phone calls you will receive will be from fast-talking agents that will tell you they have this player and are doing this or playing here and making this amount of money. However, the most important thing to remember is that your agent needs to represent you. All the other information about other players is hardly important as it relates to your career. Sure, your agent's accolades add to the validity of their work or agency, but at the end of the day, your agent needs to work hard for you and not throw around flashy numbers and names to get the job done. You need to know what the agent can and will do for you and only you. What they have going on with other players under that umbrella has nothing to do with you.

Also, after you talk to these agents, please do your homework to see how many players are represented by this potential person. To do this, you can search the agency's name and see the players represented by this particular agent. Once you do that, you can reach out to those players through social media or ask the agent to talk to them to get a better feel about signing with that agency. Usually, if you ask them something like that and there is a bit of hesitation, then there is your answer right there, telling you not to sign with that agent. Never forget that your current basketball career is your way of providing for yourself now. So, you need to ask all of the questions you may have before making the big leap of choosing an agent. This will give you a general idea if your agent is accessible when and if you need them in tough times while overseas. I often hear players say they have not talked to their agent in weeks or barely talk at all. Consider non-communication a deal-breaker because once you arrive overseas, especially at the beginning of your career, you will learn that circumstances change daily.

Lastly, do not forget that in this business, the agent works for you and not the other way around. They cannot make you take a job you do not feel comfortable with or do not want to take.

Most basketball contracts that players sign for agents to represent them all look the same. You are usually locked in with that agency for two years, and you are not allowed to do business with anyone else while represented by your agent for that time. If you decide to take a deal outside of your agency's permission, they have the right to sue you for 10% commission, which is usually the amount that the basketball club is supposed to pay to your agent that seals the deal.

These situations can get a bit messy because you can be with an agency that says they cannot find the right job for you, and someone else comes in with a job, and you take it, but the agency you are legally represented by will want that commission payment.

Suppose you are thinking about parting ways with your agency. In that case, write your agent a termination letter explaining that the agreement you signed must be terminated, effective immediately. Once that is received, signed, and submitted back to you, you can go about your business and sign with another agent. By submitting a termination letter and moving forward once that letter is signed and received, you will not encounter any lawsuits, which is the right way to do business.

Next, when considering a new agent, be sure to reach out to a few players currently represented under them and see what they have to say about their work. At times, you will be surprised by what you hear. Sometimes these situations are smoke and mirrors. One of the most important tips I recommend is sitting down and meeting with this agent in person (if possible). The eyes never lie, and in-person encounters will let you know whether this person will be a good fit for you.

Last but not least, under any circumstance, you should not accept money from any agent you talk to because this will set you up for failure and put you in debt before you receive your first paycheck from a team. During my first few years of playing pro, I played in the NBA Development League, now known as the NBA G League. During my time in the D League, I was under a C-level contract, meaning that I was making about $16k a year before taxes. I know I could have made more money working at a fast-food restaurant, but you must start somewhere as an athlete. By the way, knowing these details about my life leads to why you should not take money from an agent.

Well, at the time, I was burning through the money I earned from the D League, and once the summer came around, I was tight on cash. So, I told my former agent that I did not have any money. He told me that if I helped him pick up players from the airport and take them to workouts, he would throw me some money to hold me over since I was doing him a favor. Doing this allowed him to save money on not purchasing rental cars for the players that came and worked out with us at our training destinations. While in the city, I would work out twice a day, once playing basketball and the other with a strength trainer. We also had a physical therapist that helped us with any injuries or aches we were battling.

While all of this was taking place, I never came out of one dollar to pay for these workouts, but I received money for gas and extra money to live. Fast forward two years, and I finally realized that my career was going nowhere. I wanted to go overseas and try to earn more money. So, I sent my agent a termination letter, and he said that he was sad to see me go and wished me nothing but the best of luck with my next move and my career and that he would stay in touch. I didn't think anything of that last part because I was burned out from chasing a dream of playing in the NBA that seemed further from my grasp.

So, I signed with the agent I am currently with and never heard anything from my previous agent until I signed my first big EuroCup deal in Turkey. The email from my former agent read:

Congrats on your new deal. I knew you would be a special player in this business, and the world would eventually see what I already knew about you. However, during my time representing you, I loaned you some money, and now I know that you are in the position to pay it back. So, when you get your first check, I am going to need you to start making payments on this bill so we can get this squared away.

I read that email with smoke coming out of my ears because all I could see was a big ass number at the bottom of the email that read $22,000. I didn't know what to do! I asked myself if he could do this, but in actuality, he could and did because he had all the receipts. All I had was a verbal agreement. So, when you look at the last two years of being represented by this agent, I gave him more money than the jobs he got me.

How insane is that?

Also, when I thought back on being represented by him, he had paid for my apartment in the summer and even longer because I got cut in my first training camp and had to work out until another opportunity presented itself. Also, I had to factor in the trainers I was working with, the treatment I received, and the extra money I asked for to do things for my family and live.

I received his banking information the following month, sent his money in full, and never heard from him again. After going through that ordeal, I made sure never to take another penny from anyone, let alone another agent, because that was an expensive lesson learned. I also wanted to make sure that no one else made the same mistake. This business is very shady, and once you take that first dollar, you damned near strain the relationship with your agent. Remember, no matter how friendly your agent may seem, this is a business and money talks. If a similar opportunity presents itself, and it will because coming out of college and turning pro is a huge shift in your everyday routine, and that routine is expensive, be wiser than I once was. Once you turn pro, you eat and train differently, and those types of adjustments cost. Most of the time, your agent will have you go to a specific training facility to be evaluated, and if everything checks out, you will most likely end up staying there until you get a job. However, when you are there using all of those resources, you have to assume that none of those resources are free. Once you complete those few days of evaluation, it's time to talk about money. Do not be scared to talk about this because the last thing you want to do is dig a hole that you will find yourself trying to get out of years down the road. Make sure to understand what the agent is paying for and what you have to pay back as soon as you sign your contract. Some agents do not require their clients to pay them back because they are investing in them, and the payback will come when their clients sign big contracts. So, make sure you get something in writing and signed by the person you are dealing with because you must protect yourself and your pockets.

Chapter 2

Must-Know Contract Information

Before you sign your first professional contract, you must understand a few things before adding your signature to the dotted line. Do not let the excitement of signing a contract pull you away from ensuring that the fine print is to your benefit.

The most important thing to understand is whether you are going overseas on a "tryout" or a "fully guaranteed" contract. There is a major difference between the two. As I stated at the beginning of this book, my first deal was in Poland, but I had no idea it was a tryout until a few months into the deal. Some people are probably wondering how I did not know, but the truth is, you don't know what you don't know. Back then, I did not have resources like this book or someone to ask for advice. However, it is simple to know if your contract is fully guaranteed because you will see this under Article 1 Term in the contract that reads, *"This agreement is fully guaranteed for all salary payments in case of Player's death, injury, lack of skill, or if player becomes ill and is unable to perform."*

That one sentence should be one of the main focal points when looking over your contract. Throughout your career, there may be instances when your money is paid late or not paid at all. Importantly, having that one sentence in your contract gives you leverage when you go to court to fight for your salary for that season because the words "fully guaranteed" are nothing to play with in the court of law. When you are a fully guaranteed player, that means you are fully guaranteed to receive your money... unless the unthinkable happens and you experience payment issues with your respective club and decide to take them to court. This is a good place to mention that overseas basketball is not like the NBA, where payments are always timely and received. There are countless nightmare stories about players that never received a paycheck, only empty promises. Some clubs will terminate the existence of the basketball club in its entirety, meaning that when you file your lawsuit against them, you end up fighting against a ghost because that club no longer exists. This is an extreme measure, but this happens occasionally, and players lose out on a nice amount of money. Also, a fully guaranteed contract is null and void if you break team rules, including failing drug tests, disciplinary reasons, and so forth.

Next, make sure that airline tickets are included in your contract, not only for you but your loved ones, too, so that they can visit without having to pay for a ticket. Trust me on this. Airline tickets seem like a luxury, but they are a staple and necessary in an overseas basketball player's contract. Ticket inclusion is something you need when traveling to a foreign country. Some teams will not add tickets to your contract, which is a big red flag, but they are supposed to include at least one economy class ticket for your guest of choice. If this is not in your contract before signing, make sure you understand why it is not there or if the team will pay a stipend for you to book your family's tickets. If they provide a stipend, be sure this is in writing. Word of mouth is never sufficient.

I was introduced to the flight stipend when I signed with Alba Berlin. Initially, I was hesitant because the clubs I had played for always booked the tickets for my family and me. However, doing it this way allowed me to find the perfect ticket, and I could book the ticket when I wanted, without waiting on the team to do it on my behalf.

Once you figure out your flight situation, you want to ensure the club gives you a car, which must also be stated in your contract. I have seen and heard all kinds of stories from players having to share cars in certain countries and some not having a vehicle. I also heard of players receiving a bike, which was brutal during the winter months. You also can tell the club that you do not want a car because some people get nervous when driving in foreign places. I was this way when I played in Lebanon a few years ago. I told the team I did not want a car and would rather Uber or ride with one of my teammates to and from practice because I was too nervous about driving. If you want a vehicle, which you most likely will, make sure you make this known to your agent during contract negotiations. I don't know about you, but I know I need a car to get around and leave as I please, especially when playing in Europe. Think of grocery shopping, wanting to sightsee on your off days, or meeting up with friends. Having a car is a lot easier than figuring out a bus schedule or catching rides with teammates.

Also, you must be aware that this car is the club's property. So, this means that whatever you do to that car, the club will do to your pockets (which will affect your salary). When I was in Germany at our practice facility, we had some tight corners to maneuver to park and leave the facility. As time went on, I became comfortable with getting around and finding a parking space. However, you feel sleepy when you come from those long, late road trips because you couldn't get that much sleep on the bus. Those corners get a bit tougher to maneuver, which is exactly what happened to me. I hit the corner of our practice facility, right above the rear right wheel, trying to exit the facility to go home. I informed the team of what I did, and they took it to get serviced. Before I got my car back, I had to pay to fix it, which was about 1,700 euros. So, I stress that if you get a car for the season, treat it with care to not lose out on any money.

***

Let's switch gears and discuss packing your suitcase like a pro. When you know you will be overseas for eight to ten months, you seem to think that you must pack all your belongings in two suitcases, which will most likely be overweight, and you will have to pay for the excess weight or leave some stuff behind. I am here to tell you that you do not need most of the stuff you are about to pack. I'm sure you are probably reading this like what is he talking about, but trust me, you do not need that stuff. For starters, the majority of everything you need is already in Europe. You just don't know it yet because you have never been there. The most important things you need are two to three pairs of basketball shoes for training camp, depending on how fast you go through your shoes. Next, you need two pairs of running/walking shoes because there is a chance you may run in the mountains, on a track, or any place they can find for conditioning. I would recommend bringing all your skincare products, underwear, and cosmetics, as these items are not necessarily the same overseas. Deodorant in the States is stronger than overseas, so I always stock up on those when packing.

Depending on where you play, you may be near a military base, which is a game-changer for Americans. If you are near a military base, try to connect with one of the Americans in the military because they have stores on base with everything you get back in the States, and the items are tax-free. From your favorite cereals, candy, and seasonings (you will definitely need those), the base has it all. The only thing is that you cannot access the base unless someone from the base signs you in and gets you onto the base. I have been blessed to meet a few people from the base who have helped my family and teammates celebrate some of our favorite holidays with the food we're used to at home.

As far as clothes are concerned, what you pack depends on your country because some cities have many shops within driving distance. Personally, I like the clothes in Europe better than what I find in the States. So, when I pack, I go easy on the clothes, knowing I can shop abroad. The last thing I would want you to do is to pack the same things you can find overseas. That would be a total waste of space in your suitcase as well as a waste of money paying for bags that are overweight.

Chapter 3

Arriving in Europe

When I landed in Wroclaw, Poland, I had no idea what I was in for, let alone how to navigate the country for my rookie season. Sure, I looked some things up on the internet, but online research does not compare to anything once you're in the country. Once you get off the plane, you must go through customs. Depending on the customs staffer, the process can be short or a long, stressful experience, filled with questions and stares. I have been blessed to see both sides, which has given me more wisdom on this journey. While you wait for your bags to arrive, there may be someone from the team waiting for you to take you to your new home for the year. This person will most likely be the team manager or someone who works for the team. Chances are you will already be in contact with that person through WhatsApp, so you will already know where to meet.

After you grab your bags, there may be fans waiting outside the baggage area to welcome you to the city, depending on the club's success. These fans will want to take pictures with you and may give you a gift, too.

When I arrived in Berlin, Germany, to play with Alba Berlin, there were a few fans at the airport to greet me. I keep in contact with one fan to this very day by the name of Gabi. Gabi is awesome and a true Alba fan to the core. She has never missed my birthday, Christmas, or any other special day, always sending my family and me a special gift. When you play abroad for as long as I have, you will meet new people, and they will become loyal friends and supporters, whether you wear their team's shirt or not.

After greeting the fans, you will more than likely take a few pictures with the team's scarf, jersey, or something representing the club to announce your arrival to the city. Most likely, if you are on a guaranteed contract, the team manager will then take you to your apartment to get settled. You may not get your car on the first day because of the time you arrive (late in the evening), or the vehicle may not be ready. So, the team manager will take you to the grocery store or to a restaurant affiliated with the club for you to get food. Be careful with team managers because you will get some who are good and some who are not so great. My team manager, Roberto, from my 2020 season in Italy, was more than we could ask for, and I am forever thankful for what he did for my family. He allowed me to only think about basketball, which helped me out in many ways. My wife was working, and we had our newborn daughter with us as well. You hear many stories about when players bring their families overseas that the wives or girlfriends are sometimes left out to dry because they are not considered part of the team. This was not the case for me because Roberto took my wife and daughter to her pediatrician appointment, stayed with them the whole time, and translated what was going on so that my wife would not be in the dark. I was in practice at the time, so I could not be there. When we needed a babysitter, he found that for us, and she spoke English, too. The point is if you luck up and find a team manager that takes care of you, make sure you take care of them as well because they are rare.

After you receive your car, you should pay particular attention to how to get around the city. As you read further into this chapter, you must understand this major key: When you drive to practice, please find at least two more routes to get to practice on time. I say this because there are holidays that you do not know about, and traffic can be backed up. Also, random construction projects occur, and it just so happens that it will always be on the normal route you take to practice. When playing overseas, teams do not play about being late, so make sure you have several options for getting to the gym on time to be prepared for practice and not be financially penalized.

Next, learn the driving rules and where to park. Parking tickets and toll roads are the most dangerous things that can hurt your pockets. My wife was dropping me off at practice one day when I was playing in Venice, and she wanted to go to the city center to get coffee and enjoy the sunny day. However, as she was driving downtown, she did not realize that she was driving in an only bus lane, and the fine for doing so was 300 euros a pop. To make a long story short, I got a letter from the team stating that I had some tickets and had to pay 1,000 euros in penalties. It turned out that she had been in that lane three times in the same day. She never drove our car again.

Also, when you hear the ambulance or police sirens in America, we are trained to stop so that they can get to where they need to go. So far, whenever I hear the sirens, I immediately pull over, but I still see cars driving normally, which bothers me. However, continue to treat this as if you were at home by pulling over to give them the right of way, regardless of if people get mad.

Lastly, I want to inform you about driving abroad. When I started driving, my father always told me that I was not driving for myself but for other people, and his advice always stuck with me, especially overseas. When you are on the freeway and want to drive fast, make sure to drive in the far-left lane. As you drive in the left lane, a car may approach you at a high rate of speed. I know you are used to seeing cars switch lanes and go past you, but that is not the case in Europe. If you see the car behind you flashing their lights, this means you are going too slow and need to switch to the middle lane so they can pass you. It may sound weird, but I like this rule, and it makes sense.

Also, as it is in America, you will experience drivers with road rage. Please be careful because you must remember that you are in a foreign country where you do not speak fluent enough to get yourself out of any trouble. Also, the last thing you want to do is go to jail for getting into a fight with someone because of a misunderstanding. Be smart about this and be careful.

Chapter 4

Managing Your Money

Too often, you hear about your typical professional athlete going broke after a few years of retirement. Some even live paycheck to paycheck during their career. Well, I am here to tell you that I have seen it happen to many of my peers. However, this does not have to be you because you will have a general idea of managing the money you make during your successful career. Yes, I am speaking it into existence for you to be great.

To be honest, I was not good at managing my money, and I am still working on it as I write this book, but with the knowledge I have gained from bumping my head, plus the people I have in my corner, I trust that this information will help you. Playing professionally overseas is one of the toughest jobs you can have and saving money is even tougher. When you think about the NBA, NFL, and MLB, you know that those athletes get a pension once they surpass a consistent number of years in their respective leagues. Once you retire from playing overseas, you will *not* receive a pension. What you save is what you have once that ball stops bouncing. Some countries offer a small pension, but it is nothing compared to what the athletes receive in the United States. Suppose you happen to play all your professional years in Pro-A France (the top league in France), BBL Germany (the top league in Germany), or Serie A (the top league of Italy), you will reap some kind of money post-career. There is a catch to accessing this money, though; nonetheless, it will be there for you. You earned it! The max amount I have heard an American receiving is about $30,000. This is wonderful, but this will not hold you over for long. With that said, I want to give you some pointers on having something to show for once you retire.

  The first thing you want to do is create a budget for yourself based on your yearly salary. Once you establish your budget, you must exercise discipline. Look at all your expenses back home and plan accordingly. Try to stick to this budget for as long as possible. Often, we change our habits once the money increases. With your first job, you may not have many responsibilities besides a phone bill. So, you should be able to pocket about 90% of your salary. This may sound funny to some, but you will have the last laugh if you save diligently. Playing overseas is not about how much money you make but how much you save. Never lose track of that.

When I played in Germany, one of my teammates wanted to buy an MCM backpack. He kept talking about it when we were in the locker room. The twist to this story is that this same teammate just completed his rookie season in the G League. If you know about the G League, you know nearly half of the players overseas make a G League player's salary in one month. When I played in the G League, I thought about getting a second job to stay afloat. Well, my teammate bought the bag, but we hadn't been paid yet by our club overseas. So, I asked him how he paid for the backpack.

"I saved my money from the G League season," he replied.

My mouth dropped.

As I was processing what he said, I realized that I could have done the same thing, but I had no discipline or anyone showing me how to manage the little money I made before I started making more money. If you can't manage $50, you won't be able to manage $500. Never forget that. Anyway, I realized I was handling my money all wrong and needed help.

During your career, you will have teammates spending money on everything they may want, but that does not necessarily mean you must do the same. We live in a foreign country for eight to ten months out of the year, and we are in sweatpants most of the time anyway. We spend two to three months at home in the States, and that is when we spend the most money because we want people to know that we have it. In actuality, that is the last thing you should do. I have been guilty of doing this, of overspending, but I grew out of that fast. So, when you come home for the summer, I recommend *not* buying a car if you don't own one. Buying a car makes no sense at all because that car will sit in your garage for the remainder of the year. After all, you will be overseas. Instead, I recommend going to a rental car service and paying for the rental car while at home. That way, you are not liable for any maintenance, and the only thing you must do is pay for insurance unless you have some already. Once you sign that overseas contract, drop the keys off at Enterprise and go on about your business. No strings attached.

The next major expense involves getting a place to stay. Where you choose to stay depends on your situation, but I recommend finding a fully furnished apartment for the summer if it is just you. Most of the time, you will buy some nice things that you may not be able to take overseas with you. So, there are storage units where you can store your things for the time being until you find a home of your own at the right time. Once it's time to go back overseas, drop the keys off to the owner of your rental and become worry-free from any responsibilities that come with owning a home.

During those two to three months of being in America, be sure to enjoy a vacation. Importantly, make sure you are budgeting for this during your season. My wife and I go somewhere every year once I complete my season. It is one of the highlights of my year because I get to relax and decompress from basketball. I enjoy spending my money on this, and we get our money's worth from these trips. Traveling is what I like, and I understand that you may like something else. The thing is, you worked hard for whatever you chose to spend your money on, so you might as well enjoy yourself but do not go overboard and hurt your pockets.

Speaking of money, I wanted to save this topic for the end of this chapter because I need you to remember this important lesson. Just because the basketball club pays your taxes while playing in their country does not mean you do not have to file your taxes in the United States. You must file your taxes in the United States no matter what anyone tells you. Filing taxes is vital because tax issues are an overseas athlete's worst nightmare regarding purchasing a home or other major investment. Also, you do not want the IRS coming after you because they will bleed you dry. Some states do not have a state tax, such as Texas, Florida, and Nevada, but you must also file federal taxes. I cannot stress this enough. You can ask the club for the bank statements to have a paper trail of what has been deposited into your account. From there, you can pass those statements to the person who does your taxes but make sure you stay on top of this because your taxes are not the team's issue. When you hear an overseas athlete say they make $100k tax-free, just know that they must file that $100k once it is time to file their taxes in the United States.

A friend of mine, a first-time homebuyer, was so happy to purchase his home. After all, he worked his butt off to get to that point. Once he got all his information together and it was time to take the next step with the housing process, he realized he owed back taxes. With this taking place, his dream home was on halt for the time being until he took care of his situation with Uncle Sam. Once he got his tax issue situated, he was approved for his home, and his home is very nice, I must say. However, his dream almost did not come true due to not knowing about filing his taxes on the money he earned overseas. I do not want this to be you. Once you finish your season, be sure to file your taxes so you can get your dream home, too.

Chapter 5

Let's Talk Money

Imagine working in a foreign country for nine months and being isolated from most of your family, and when you look back at the experience, you've only been paid for six of those nine months. I want to be very transparent on what you could face while playing overseas because I can guarantee that every athlete that has played overseas will have a story about their career or someone else not being paid in full. Most of the time, when it comes to playing basketball overseas, you can expect your money to be late at some point throughout the season. When you look at your contract, it will have a specific date of getting paid. However, I am here to tell you to expect the unexpected. Many factors go into this equation to getting your salary on time or receiving it at all.

First, when you begin your career, do not panic when you do not get paid the first payment. Knowing what I know now, I tell most young guys to consider their rookie season as an investment. I am not telling you to play for free. You will know when to talk with your agent and figure out the next move, but if your payment is two to three weeks late, continue to handle the basketball side of the job and let your agent handle the dirty work. Also, some clubs have money issues and are nervous to tell you because of their good history with paying players on time. The number one thing in this whole equation is communication but more so how you communicate. Again, allow your agent to handle financial situations. The moment you approach management, your team's staff may be quick to call you problematic or try to ruin your reputation.

Next, you have some clubs that blatantly just don't care if the money is late and dare you to go to court about it. Stay away from those clubs. Today, with the power of social media and the internet, you can do more research on these teams and reach out to former players to see how they were treated while on the team offering you a contract. Ultimately, after you hear about their experiences, whether good or bad, the choice is up to you at the end of it all because you are the person that has to live with that decision. I have played on teams where some guys told me the experience was bad for them and they did not receive their money at times, but my experience with the team was completely different from theirs. I always trusted my gut and my agent to never steer me wrong during this process. We have been blessed in this department of the business. However, just because your agent tells you it is a good situation does not mean that's the case. Never forget that you are the one overseas playing and living, not your agent. Most of the time, when playing in Germany and France, you will rarely hear about an athlete being paid late. There are also some clubs in Spain, Turkey, Russia, Italy, and Poland that pay on the actual date of the payment. During my 2020-2021 season in Italy, I was often paid a week before my payment date, definitely not mad at them at all.

 Next, get familiar with team fines. At the beginning of the season, most likely, you will receive a few sheets of paper upon arrival with the "rules" for the season. It usually goes like this: If you are late to the bus, practice, or games, receive a technical foul, are disrespectful to management, or are out of dress code during team breakfast, lunch, or dinner, you will be assessed a fine. When playing in Europe, you must realize that it is something like a family, a brotherhood, and no one is above the next person. Everyone is expected to hold each other accountable, so when management asks you to wear something, please just do it and go on about your day.

My former teammate and I were in the airport in St. Petersburg, Russia, waiting to board our flight back home. We had just lost a tough game, but our ranking was still good in the EuroCup. However, the management was not happy about the loss. We had played a league game on the road before departing to Russia. So, our team travel polos were dirty, and I wore another shirt, and so did my teammate. As we sat in the airport, eating and playing cards, the team manager told us we would be fined if we did not put on the team polo while traveling. We told him that the polo was under the plane with our luggage. He said okay and walked off. We didn't think anything of it, but the following month, once we saw that our payment was off by 1,000 euro, we went to the office and talked with the manager. We asked him why our salaries were short, and he told us we were fined for not following the dress code. From that point on, I wore that polo everywhere, even on off days sometimes.

The next topic is bonuses in your contract. Most of the time, your bonuses are negotiable. Also, let me make this clear: Everyone on your team does not have the same bonus structure, so be mindful of who you talk with about this. Your bonuses and your contract are your business and your business only. If you can, keep the details to yourself because people talk more than they should, and you do not want your business floating around like that. One guy playing in EuroLeague might make it to the finals and earn $50,000, but his teammate, on the other hand, would earn $10,000. Both amounts are nice pieces of change, but if I had my pick, I would pick 50 over ten every day of the week.

This last topic I need you to pay close attention to and make your decisions wisely. As you chase the dream of being a professional athlete, I will never tell you to turn down any money. I want to see you maximize your potential to the fullest and get every dollar possible. However, what I will tell you is never to chase the money. People often see huge deals that their agents bring to them, but things are not always what they seem. When playing overseas, there is something called *image contracts*.

You will usually see these contracts once you are already in the country you will be playing in. This contract will be different from what you signed while home in your respective country, but it must be signed to get paid your full salary for the season. An image contract allows the basketball clubs to pay you less because the money comes from a separate party and the pay dates are usually different from what the team pays you. Do not be alarmed about this once you see it, but just be aware that you will receive two different payments on your pay day. I have played on teams and dealt with image contracts and have been blessed to get all my money. However, other people have not been as lucky.

I remember when I was in full negotiations with teams, preparing for the following season, and I received a big offer from a club in Italy. We were in talks with this club in previous years, but I went another route, so this time, they made sure to get my attention, which they did to a certain extent. It was a $400,000 deal, base salary, but the bonus structure was amazing. I'll put it like this – if we finished in eighth place for the regular season, I would receive $50,000 in bonus money just for making the playoffs. As you're reading this, you probably assumed I took the deal.

Well, you're wrong.

I passed on that deal and signed in Germany to play with Alba Berlin. Before, I told you to make sure not to chase the money. Many times, when you chase the money, you tend to get stuck because you see the dollar signs. The situation may be bad for you, or you are held back from being the player they told you they wanted you to be before you signed the deal. You must be careful with all these variables. All of that money this club was offering me was coming from an image contract, but what you might not know is that it is difficult to sue a club when your money is in an image contract.

I followed my gut, and it worked out in my favor because, during that season, that club got hit with a few lawsuits, causing players to find new teams. It's good to earn what you believe you are worth or because you worked your butt off but be aware of what you sign and make sure the situation makes sense for you.

Chapter 6

Protecting Yourself

Have you ever heard of the saying, "It's better to have it and not need it than to need it and not have it"?

There have been several times when I've gotten into it with my teammates at lunch when talking about health insurance and not depending on the team to cover you. Yes, when you pass your physical with your club, you become fully insured under the basketball club for the duration of your contract while *in their country*. However, the question I've always had for my teammates and people I talk to about this is what happens when you are home in the summer.

We play all year round, and when we are home, we often play in different leagues or tournaments, especially so our family and friends can see us since they may not have had a chance to while we played overseas. Also, you have workouts to prepare you for the next season. The point I'm trying to make is that anything can happen at any given time. I pray that nothing happens to you in Jesus' name, but why not protect your main source of income, your body, from any injury that could happen? When you have your own insurance, this allows you to get second opinions on an injury diagnosis that you may have questioned. One thing to be mindful of is when you are playing for a professional organization, the team doctor works for the team, not you. So, the best way to prevent anything sketchy from taking place is to have your own doctor in the States where you can send your results and make your decision from there.

When I played in China, I went up for a lay-up off an offensive rebound. The defender swiped down as we all do, but this time he hit my hand, and I felt something pop. With my adrenaline pumping, I figured I just jammed my finger. So, I yanked it and tried to continue playing the game. As I ran down the floor, I was feeling a strong, throbbing beat in my hand. So, I looked at the coach and signaled for him to take me out of the game. I couldn't move my right index finger, and there was a small bump on top of my hand. After the game, they took me to the doctor and performed a few X-rays. Once they finished with the examination, they took me to another room and showed me the X-rays. The doctor told me that it was too early to tell what was going on because of the swelling in my hand. However, I knew something wasn't right. So, I took out my phone, got the best pictures possible, and sent them to my doctor back in the States.

The next morning, my doctor and agent called me and said that I broke my metacarpal in my index finger and needed surgery. My mouth dropped because the doctor in China told me that the X-ray was not good enough to see because of the swelling. To make a long story short, I left the team since I couldn't play anymore and went home to get the surgery. Thankfully, I had my own insurance, so I didn't handicap myself depending on the team. At the end of the day, the team will most likely look out for the team, not your well-being. Not to say that every team doctor will do that to you, but an inaccurate diagnosis is no surprise when it does take place.

I paid for the surgery, which was about $1,200 after my deductible, and I was home recovering. Think how much surgery, rehab, and anesthesia would have cost me if I didn't have my own health insurance. I would have been looking at about $25,000 out of pocket. This is why I stress to overseas athletes to get health insurance. Today, I pay $351 a month for insurance. I have my bill set on auto-pay, and I never lose an ounce of sleep about it because I know that if I ever had an ill feeling or question about something, I could make an appointment with my doctor and get right.

Every year, once the season is over, I schedule a physical with my doctor before resuming basketball activities in the summer to know that I am healthy. Also, I see my chiropractor at least once a month to ensure that my body is aligned properly. Next, I have my physical therapist to help with any issue I may have with my body. This is my team that I have to ensure that my body is at its peak performance when I step on that court. All of this is possible and affordable because of having insurance.

Lastly, let's discuss surgery. Many American athletes do not feel comfortable going under the knife overseas, but they leave themselves no choice when they don't have insurance in the States. This is one of the worst feelings in the world, and it happens often. Please do not get me wrong, some doctors overseas are the best at what they do, and some people come out even better after surgery. Personally, if I had to go under the knife, I would want to do it in the comforts of my decision and rest in my home in the States.

You might be thinking that what I spend monthly on my insurance is a bit much. However, I am spending the same amount protecting myself and my peace of mind as you will spend on a pair of sneakers. Which is more important to you?

Chapter 7

Overseas Basketball

When I finally decided to go overseas to play, my entire outlook on the game changed. I've learned so much from playing abroad that I do not think I would be the player I am today had I not experienced years overseas. The game is evolving, and we see more European athletes making their mark in the game. Playing overseas will probably be the best atmosphere you play in during your career unless you are playing in game seven of the NBA Finals. I've been blessed to play in some hostile and intense games overseas, and playing back at home has nothing on that type of environment.

First, you must understand that the fans are not conservative, relaxed, and just watching the game. Think about the "Cameron Crazies" section at Duke University but with the whole arena screaming and chanting in one accord. Think about a whole section of people walking around wearing their team's colors or with paint on their chest, already drunk or high off something just to help their team get that extra edge to win the game. Or, to go even further, imagine playing in a game, and seeing smoke in the arena, but no one is panicking because someone lit a flare, which is common. Now you see a big red cloud of smoke that symbolizes your team's colors, and you must play like nothing is abnormal. That is basketball overseas in some countries.

I've been on the other side of fan support, and things were not in my favor. I remember playing in Israel during the playoffs against our rivals, Maccabi Holon. To give you a heads up, this was my first time playing in the playoffs in my career, so I was super hype about it. We were playing at home, and it was game three of the playoffs. Our team had been battling back and forth in games one and two, resulting in us winning one game on the road. We would've swept them if it wasn't for an altercation that took place with my teammate's wife and child while watching our game. My teammate's wife and child were attacked in the stands as we tried to make it to the locker room for halftime. This is a whole different story, and it hits different now that I have a daughter of my own. Truthfully, nobody was thinking about the game because we were worried about the mother and her child's well-being, so the club had them sit in the locker room with us for the time being, and we took that loss across the chin. All I remember was one of my favorite teammates and leaders that I shared a floor with, Jeremis Smith, having a conversation with us that held no cut cards: "I don't think you guys understand how important each game is," he explained. "All I see is whoever scored the ball celebrating and shit but not getting back on defense. In my years of playing professionally, I have never not made it to the final four, and I will be damned if I start this year. Let me see another one of you celebrating after a made basket, and you will deal with me. And I can assure you that not a damn soul in this locker room can get me off you."

Jeremis was a proven winner and a great leader. After that conversation, we locked in and closed out the series.

Regarding game three at home, we made big play after big play. During the game, as I was taking the ball out under the basket, the opposing team's "rowdy" fans were behind me. As the ref handed me the ball, I noticed my teammate giving me this weird look, peering at my shoulder. Well, one of the fans spat on my shoulder, and once I realized it, I dropped the ball and turned around to see who did it. I was livid, and the ref grabbed me and told me not to go into the stands because it would incite a riot. Let me remind you that we were the home team; we outnumbered them, so I loved the odds. I also think spitting on someone is the ultimate sign of disrespect. My teammate, Tony Younger, calmed me down because I had never experienced anything like that in my playing career. Through it all, we won the game and eventually closed them out in game four, and I will have those memories forever. Even though that took place early in my career, I still say that playing overseas has the best playing atmosphere ever, and I stand on that.

Next, you must learn how to control your emotions with the referees. Most of the time, when Americans go overseas to play, we have to adjust to the new rules and the style of play. We always get called for traveling because we take that first step before putting the ball on the ground, or we get called for traveling when we do a spin move in the lane as a counter to the defender cutting us off. Things are starting to change with the rules, but you still must be careful about those two moves. When dealing with the referees, the most important thing is controlling your emotions when calls don't go your way, which is easier said than done. I'm sure you've heard the saying "control what you can control," and I tried using that mantra, but sometimes I just need to get what I have to say off my chest, and the refs do not like it. They think that the fans pay to watch them control a game. The last thing you want to do, especially in Europe, is get labeled in a bad way because it will be a very long season for you, and it ends up hurting your team. When you sign overseas, you are often the primary focus of the team. So, if you are more focused on the refs than helping your team, it leads to nothing but trouble for you and your club.

Lastly, the warm-up leading to the game is basically a mini-game before the actual game starts. Before I made the jump overseas, I was playing in the NBA D League. We would go to the court for warm-ups with about 12 minutes left on the clock. Before that time, we would have our time slot on the court with about two to three other players to get our shots up and do our pre-game routines. However, we knew that we would run out together when that clock hit 12 and warm up as a team before starting the game. Playing overseas is a complete 180 of what I did in the States. Remember, my first official game in Poland was at home against our rival team, Anwil, and the atmosphere was electric. So, you know I was ready to play in the game once I walked into the gym wearing my street clothes. When we ran out, our crowd went crazy. We separated into our traditional lay-up lines, and off the rip, everyone started dunking and going crazy. About five to seven minutes in, I was drenched in sweat and ready for the game. As I looked at the time on the clock, the time read 20:00. So, I stopped and asked my European teammate what was going on. He told me that we were about to start warming up. Meanwhile, I was already warm warm! To make a long story short, once we started the game, I caught a cramp after two minutes and had to be subbed out. I never warmed up that hard again since I've been playing in Europe.

Chapter 8

Mental Health

This subject of mental health has just started to be discussed more, yet it has been in existence forever. I tell people all the time that I compare playing overseas to deploying abroad. I say that because you go to a foreign country for a long period. You adjust and adapt to their culture, learn their way of living, learn their language, and are over there for so long that you become shell shocked once you come back home to the States. I've been blessed to play this game overseas for ten years, and I am still playing, but to be honest, I feel more comfortable overseas than at home. A big part of that could be because I have been home for a grand total of 14 months (not counting the surgery recovery time from December 2019 to September 2020). So, I hope you understand that I am more comfortable overseas because I have been living in Europe for over a decade of my life. As time goes on, you will miss out on making many memories, such as your loved ones' weddings, birthdays, graduations, and funerals. Missing those events is something you must sacrifice when chasing this dream. There will never be a perfect story to this basketball grind, but this is what makes everyone's story so unique once they choose to share it with someone. Many people think it's so easy to go overseas to play and make money because they see what we post on social media, but they have no idea about the bullshit that we go through behind the scenes.

Here is one example: I played in China in the summer of 2017. I had just come off a great year in Italy with Pallacanestro Varese. Originally, I told my agent that I wanted to give the NBA another shot after the short season in China, so I would not sign with any team in Europe. However, Umana Reyer Venezia came into the picture, and they had just won the Italian Championship. When playing in these countries, I have always been good individually but not as much collectively with my team. So, I looked at this opportunity as a chance to compete for a championship. Talking to the coach made me feel as if I was the missing piece for them to repeat as champions, and I liked the team they were building. So, I took the deal, and it was for a nice amount of money as well. I was gone the previous year, and my wife and I talked about taking a break from her job to be overseas with me in Venice, Italy.

Sounds like an ideal situation, right?

Playing for that coach was the worse decision of my career. The coach wanted me on the team because of my scoring ability, and when he took that away from me, I went into a downward spiral. There were times I would score back-to-back baskets, and then he would sub me out. Or, I would make a defensive mistake, and he would take me out. Meanwhile, I checked out mentally with him because I couldn't trust him, and more importantly, I started doubting myself. I would become frustrated, but he never gave me a real answer to the issue or problem he had with me. As time went on, I stopped playing because the club kept bringing in new players (Americans). So, in Italy, the rule is you must have the same number of locals (Italians) as foreign players. We had 13 guys on our team, so there would always be an odd man out, me. I would ask him what's going on, and he would tell me that I demanded too much attention when I stepped on the floor, and I took away from what the team was trying to accomplish.

Whatever the hell that meant.

Bottom line, I went into a small form of depression because I had my wife out there with me, and we were supposed to be enjoying life together, but I felt like I wasn't doing my job since I couldn't be myself out on the court. I also felt bad because she left a great-paying job to allow me to follow my dream, but it seemed like we were just on a paid vacation, and I didn't like that at all. My wife told me that she knew what I was going through, and she let me have my space before I lost my mind. I couldn't wait to go home, and I didn't care about the money they were paying me because I was miserable.

Now that I am wiser, I can catch these feelings before they get out of hand, but I also put more effort into talking to my wife and close friends when life gets shaky. When you play overseas, you must have a support system back home to truly confide in and call you out on your bullshit. This creates a healthy balance, and life will go much smoother with basketball and everyday living. Just because you make a substantial amount of money, most of your so-called friends won't tell you when they see something wrong on your end because they think you will cut them off. However, I am here to tell you that those are not your friends. Those are leeches, and you need to get rid of them before you start making the big bucks because the problems will only get bigger as your salary increases.

Also, you must be aware of how important each game is when you play overseas. You will play about 30 games each season, and every one of those games counts no matter what the coaching staff or club tries to tell you. So, I advise you to stay mentally healthy and find a hobby outside of basketball because the worst thing you can do after a loss is come home to an empty apartment and dwell on the loss or your bad performance. I've repeatedly dwelled on both because I'm a competitor, and competitors want to do well, but sometimes, players have bad games. There are video games, reading, meditating, and going out with friends but be careful with partying after a loss.

I picked up the 24-hour rule from the head coach of the women's basketball team of the University of South Carolina,

Dawn Staley. Whether I win or lose, I have 24 hours to dwell on it, and once those 24 hours pass, I'm on to the next thing. This helped me so much last season. So, I shared this with my teammates, and that rule helped them as well. This was a major help for my mental stability because I hate losing just like the next person.

    The next issue is when we get those disturbing phone calls from our family and friends back at home in the States. It was Friday, February 13, 2015, and I was in Tarnobrzeg, Poland, sitting in my small apartment talking to one of my childhood friends named Quez, whom I viewed as a brother. We were talking about the outfit he was trying to buy for Valentine's Day. I remember the conversation vividly because, sadly, that would be the last one we ever had. As we were typing messages back and forth on Facebook messenger, and I was trying to give him some pointers on the European swag to switch his style up, I noticed that the message bubble was bouncing on the screen. I knew he was typing, but suddenly, the bubble disappeared, and nothing came through. It was about 2 am back in Detroit, Michigan, and it was 8 am where I was. I was getting ready for practice, but I was waiting on his message to see what he thought about the outfit I suggested. Still, nothing came through, and I left for morning practice.

Practice was good, just like any other day. We got some shots up and lifted weights, but the real practice was later that night because I was getting ready to play against my former team the next day, Slask Wroclaw, and they were ranked second in the league. I arrived back at my apartment, and my dad called me and said he thought that something had happened to Quez, but he didn't know for sure. Not thinking the worst, I assumed Quez did something funny because he's goofy, so I called him but didn't get an answer. A few minutes later, my dad called again and told me that Quez was dead from a gunshot wound to the head. A so-called friend was in his home with him, and that person ended up taking Quez's life by shooting him in the head. I lost it and couldn't keep myself together. However, being overseas alone with no one to be with you in a time of need weighs on you differently. You feel isolated because that's exactly what you are—alone.

That day, I arrived at practice with tears in my eyes. My American teammates knew what had happened because they were all I had over there at the time, so I had already told them. Then, I told the coach what had happened. Mind you, I mentioned we had a huge game coming up, but once I told him about my friend getting killed and crying in front of him, his next response was, "You're still going to play in the game, right?" The last thing I was thinking about was the game because I was ready to fly home to be with my friends and family, but my agent's daughter calmed me down and said something to me that made me relax: "Play in honor of your friend. That's what he would want you to do," she said.

Quez loved football, and out of all my friends, I was the one who made it and achieved the dream of being a professional athlete. So, before the game, they held a moment of silence for Quez to remember him, and I sent the video to the family back at home. After the video, it was time to play the game, and I had my best game professionally up to that point. Our team shot 27/27 from the free-throw line, which rarely happens. I only missed two shots that game and finished with 33 points. Shots that I knew were off went in, and I would just look up and smile because I knew Quez was there with me.

I will never forget that game, but those tragedies are some of the issues we go through overseas, and you are left with no choice but to deal with them. Coping is never easy, but we do it. No matter how cheesy or lame it sounds, never have too much pride not to talk to someone when going through personal battles, especially when isolated overseas. It may be a long shot, but I am here for you because almost everything you will experience overseas, I have already been through it or seen it. So, I will do my damn best to give solid advice on your situation so you avoid anything that can harm you or your career, and I stand on that.

Chapter 9

Leisure

Once you are finally settled in your city and start to figure out a schedule for yourself, it's time to venture out and see what your city and surrounding countries have to offer. Many people would love to be in your shoes, so you must take advantage of the opportunities presented to you, including exploring a new place. Something I regretted during my rookie season while playing in Wroclaw, Poland, is that I never went anywhere when I had free time. I was so locked in on the actual job that I missed opportunities to see the country. Europe is a beautiful place, and you will make memories to have forever. So, I urge you to find out how to catch a train out there, travel to another city, sightsee, and relax to take your mind off the sport for a day or two when the time presents itself. Once my wife started to travel abroad to see me, she had a list of things that she wanted us to see, and I'm thankful for her doing that because I am completely the opposite with taking pictures and planning sightseeing trips. Thanks to her, we now have photo albums in almost every country that I've played in, and now we can share those pictures with our family and friends who didn't get the opportunity to visit me while I was abroad.

Next, there's shopping overseas, which is one of my favorite things to do over there, especially when I lived near Milan, Paris, and Florence. Now, I see that everyone is into all the high-end designer brands, but these have been in existence for a long time. Shopping is therapeutic in a way, especially when I'm stressed after a tough practice. This may sound crazy, but I do not buy much of anything in the States anymore because I have everything I need overseas. I haven't bought a pair of basketball shoes in over three years in the States. Enjoy browsing the stores, check out the fashion, learn about other cultures, and don't stop yourself from trying new things.

These last two subjects are very important, and you must be careful in every way you can. As crazy as it may sound, you will not experience a club vibe like Europe. Some countries are more fun than others, and just to name a few, you have Tel Aviv (Israel), Milan (Italy), Paris (France), Athens (Greece), and Berlin (Germany). Some clubs play strictly hip hop and R&B, and you will have the time of your life. However, you must be careful because some teams will have "spotters" in the club to see if one of their players is there, especially after a loss or a bad game. You must be very professional about this and choose wisely when you go out to relax or have fun. The worst thing you can do as an athlete over there is drive to the club, get drunk, and get pulled over with the team's logo all over your car. This makes the basketball club looks bad, and this is when the rumors start to circulate that you are only there to party and do not take your job seriously.

In Turkey, my teammates and I were in a club in Istanbul, having a good time. We had our section, but only two people were drinking, and some women were drinking the rest. As time went on, the drinks kept coming, and as the drinks kept coming, the bill continued to increase. As time went on, I asked my friend if he was okay and needed anything toward the bill. He said no, so I told everyone to be safe, and then I left the club.

The next morning, I received a call from someone at the club, telling me that they were going to call our basketball club because we walked out without paying the bill. Those types of problems are something you must avoid when you go out because some of these basketball clubs do not want you out anyways, but we still do it. So, I found out how much the bill was, paid it, and got the money from the guys later that week. But this could've ended badly, and there is no telling what the penalty would have been for us had they made that call.

The last thing is about women, and this is the most important topic in this chapter. There is no secret about it that the women in Europe are very attractive for the most part, but you must be careful with who you choose or who chooses you. Behind every successful man is a strong woman that has his back through everything. In this scenario, when you go to these clubs, lounges, and bars, and they know you are an American, you automatically have an X on your back, and sometimes, those feelings are reciprocated. However, the thing that most Americans get messed up on is that the woman they choose to talk to usually has an ex-boyfriend in the vicinity.

There was a guy playing in Romania, and he was at a club one evening. Well, a girl came up to him and took his hat off and put it on her head. In some countries, this symbolizes that the woman likes you or finds you attractive. Meanwhile, as she did this, a guy she talked to was in the club with his friends, and they saw this occur. One thing led to another, and the American ended up being stabbed several times, resulting in him losing his life. I'm not saying that all stories end up like this, but if you go out and enjoy yourself, make sure you know the full story with these women before you make any decisions. There are some positive stories about meeting women overseas, and some people end up finding their soulmates. These are always good stories to hear, but in most situations, the bad outweighs the good.

To close this chapter out, I need you to understand that while you are overseas, people will stare at you. At first, their stares will make you uncomfortable. It sure made me feel that way my first time overseas. I was standing with a group of my teammates, and a random guy kept looking at me. So, I looked back, being an asshole, and the guy straight up asked me if I was from Africa. I was thrown off when he asked because that was the last thing I expected, but he was truly curious. He said he had never seen anyone with my complexion. We stood there and talked for a minute, and I explained to him where I was from, and we were cool after that. However, I know that some of you reading this may not have the patience I have with people, and that conversation could have gone left very quickly.

Overall, playing overseas is a fun and fascinating experience, and I would not change my profession for the world. I just want to make sure that you can avoid some of the hiccups that I have experienced or witnessed, and I feel it is my job to warn and prepare you for them before they are presented to you.

Chapter 10

Extras

In this last chapter, I figured I would leave you with something to help make your transition of living overseas a little less stressful. One of the things that I wished I would have done from the beginning of traveling overseas was to travel on the same airline as much as possible. I am talking about joining a frequent flyer club with one of your favorite airlines that you enjoy flying on while in the States. Now, I have two accounts, one of which is with Turkish Airlines who is partnered with United Airlines, and the other one, which is my favorite, is Sky Team, partnered through Delta Airlines. Once you accumulate so many points from flying on the same airlines, the benefits start to show, and then you can upgrade seats to something more comfortable. Or they will automatically do it for you because of your status. I've been traveling all around the world for ten strong years. Imagine if I flew on the same airline this whole time and what I could do with those frequent flyer miles. So, if I were you, once you sign with a team, I would let your agent know that you want to fly on a specific airline. Then, find the best, affordable ticket you can and send it to the team so they can take care of it for you.

Next, you have options of a travel rewards credit card. Having one of these credit cards can be very beneficial while living overseas because you get a chance to build your credit and rack up points that can help you with travel expenses. While overseas, I have often experienced going up to the counter, using my debit card, and getting hit with a foreign transaction fee since I was out of the country. With a travel rewards card from whoever you bank (I am more familiar with Bank of America and Chase), you have the opportunity to have those foreign transaction fees waived once you reach a certain level with your saving and spending. Also, some places overseas do not accept American Express, but every country takes Visa. A travel rewards card is usually a Visa, so I recommend looking into this, making it happen, and seizing the opportunity to build your credit while using your card.

Another thing I quickly realized while playing overseas was that I hated the televisions that the teams had for me in my place. While I was playing in Turkey, my teammate had this big box shipped to him from his former team in Greece. It was a television, and I wondered when he bought it. He told me that he bought it a few years back, and it made him feel like he was at home while watching sporting events or just playing video games. So, that very next year, I went to the electronics store and got myself a 60-inch flat-screen, and it has been to every country that I've played in up until now. I would recommend making sure that you take good care of the box for shipping purposes. Once that box is beat up, you do not want to ship that television anymore because it is fragile.

Also, don't forget about the military bases near you. I talked about this in Chapter Two, but I will go into more details about it now. I look at the military base as a taste of home whenever I get the opportunity to get on one because they have everything you are used to at home, and you must use USD when purchasing. They have almost all of the good restaurants on the base that you love back home as well. My first time going to the base was when I was playing for Umana Reyer Venezia. Man, that Thanksgiving was one of the best I had in a long time because I got to eat the food I was used to growing up, thanks to my good friend Legend (R.I.P.). I met Legend through one of my teammates at Venezia. Legend always looked out for us whenever we needed anything. He was at all our home games and even some road ones too. Unfortunately, Legend passed away at the end of my season with Venezia, and he is missed dearly. I am still shocked about him passing away at an early age, but I know he is watching over me as I write about him. So, once you get to your team, search on Facebook or Instagram to see if you are close to a base and connect with someone over there. They love to chop it up with other Americans and come to a game or two if you give them tickets.

    Last but certainly not least, you have nothing but time on your hands when you are overseas, depending on how crazy your coach is with the practices and rest times. For the people leaving school early to pursue this dream of being a professional athlete, make sure you complete your degree while in the groove of studying. I learned the hard way, but to be honest, I had never been more focused at this age than I was when the education was free. While in school, I thought the main reason I was in school was to play basketball, and once the season was over, I stopped going. If you are one semester or one year away from getting your degree, I encourage you to enroll in online courses from your university and get it done. One of my biggest accomplishments was walking across that stage and having my parents, wife, and unborn child witness it. Receiving that degree felt better than any championship I have ever won, and I would hate for you to let all the time you spent in college go to waste. If you need a tutor, find one. The worst thing you can do is make excuses for this when you know that you can do anything you put your mind to achieve. I stopped making excuses and got it done, and I want you to do the same. I bet you wouldn't go half speed on the basketball court, so do not do that with the classroom. My father told me they could take basketball away from me, but they could not take away my degree. I earned that, and it's mine.

Conclusion

Throughout life, there will be bumps in the road because ups and downs are normal. One of the main reasons I decided to write this book is to get this information out from my past experiences and make sure that whoever is coming up behind me has some type of blueprint on approaching this game in the right way. Sure, you will make mistakes as we all do, but with the information in this book, I hope those mistakes can be as minimal as possible. I wish I had this information available when I first started the overseas grind. I can only imagine how much different life would be for me as well as my family. However, this is the journey God decided for me, and I would not have written this book for you to follow for your benefit. So, it all worked out just the way it was supposed to, and I wish you nothing but the best on your professional journey. Go be great!

www.ingramcontent.com/pod-product-compliance
Lightning Source LLC
Chambersburg PA
CBHW070326100426
42743CB00011B/2577